STEPHEN SPARROW

DRIVING SALES SECRETS
UNVEILED
USING APPS & CHATBOTS
AUTOMATION

WHATSAPP

MARKETING

FOR

GROWTH

I am really thrilled that you have decided to embark on this journey of digital marketing with me. By the way, I'm Stephen Sparrow, a marketing expert with a passion for staying on the cutting edge of industry trends. With many years of experience in the field, I have successfully led numerous businesses to harness the potential of WhatsApp marketing.

As a recognized thought leader in the realm of digital marketing, I've not only embraced emerging technologies but has also played an active role in helping businesses adapt and thrive in the dynamic landscape of WhatsApp marketing.

My dedication to user privacy and data protection has earned me a reputation for ethical and responsible marketing practices. I am committed to sharing my expertise to help businesses leverage the power of WhatsApp for connecting with their audience, driving engagement, and achieving remarkable results.

In addition to my practical experience, I'm an advocate for continuous learning and innovation. I'm a sought-after speaker at marketing conferences and a contributor to industry publications, sharing my insights on WhatsApp marketing and the evolving digital landscape.

I believes that successful marketing is built on a foundation of trust, personalization, and delivering value to the audience. This book reflects my commitment to helping businesses navigate the complexities of WhatsApp marketing with integrity, effectiveness, and a vision for the future.

Stephen Sparrow

(Author)

WhatsApp Marketing Techniques for Growth: **Driving Sales Secrets Unveiled**

Table of Contents

Compliance and Privacy, Staying Compliant with WhatsApp Policies, User Privacy and Data Protection, GDPR and WhatsApp Marketing

Chapter 11
Troubleshooting and Problem Solving, Common Challenges in WhatsApp Marketing, Solutions for Technical and Engagement Issues, Dealing with Unsubscribers and Negative Feedback

Chapter 12
Future Trends and Innovations,
Predictions for the Future of WhatsApp Marketing, Preparing for Emerging Technologies, Staying Ahead of the Curve

Conclusion
Recap of Key Notes, Your Roadmap to WhatsApp Marketing Success

In today's digital age, where connectivity and instant communication are paramount, WhatsApp has emerged as a powerful platform for businesses to engage with their customers. WhatsApp Marketing, the practice of using this widely adopted messaging app for business purposes, offers a direct and personal way to connect with your audience.

Why WhatsApp Marketing Matters

WhatsApp Marketing matters for several compelling reasons. First and foremost, it boasts a user base of over two billion people worldwide, making it one of the most popular messaging apps on the planet. Its end-to-end encryption ensures the security of conversations, which in turn builds trust between businesses and customers. Furthermore, its multimedia capabilities, including text, images, videos, and documents, provide an array of options for creative and informative marketing.

WhatsApp is where your customers are, and if you're not there too, you're missing out on valuable opportunities for engagement, customer satisfaction, and, ultimately, sales growth. It's a platform that bridges the gap between businesses and their target audience, and mastering WhatsApp Marketing can be a game-changer for your marketing strategy.

What to Expect from This Book

In this ebook, we'll take you on a journey through the world of WhatsApp Marketing. We'll explore the essential techniques, strategies, and secrets that will help you drive sales, boost engagement, and make the most of this dynamic communication channel. Whether you're a small business owner, a marketing professional, or anyone interested in harnessing the power of WhatsApp for business, this ebook is your comprehensive guide to success.

Each chapter will provide you with valuable insights, practical tips, and real-world examples to help you leverage WhatsApp Marketing effectively. From setting up your WhatsApp Business account to crafting compelling messages, running campaigns, and staying compliant with policies, we've got you covered. By the time you finish reading this ebook, you'll be well-equipped to unlock the potential of WhatsApp Marketing and drive your business towards growth.

So, let's launch fully into and uncover the secrets of WhatsApp Marketing that will lead to increased sales and a stronger connection with your audience. Your journey to WhatsApp Marketing success starts here.

Chapter 1

Setting the Stage

In the world of marketing, every successful campaign begins with a solid foundation. Before you can effectively utilize WhatsApp as a marketing tool, it's crucial to set the stage. We'll go through the power of WhatsApp for business, the significance of understanding your audience, and the importance of defining clear marketing goals.

The Power of WhatsApp for Business

WhatsApp, originally developed as a simple messaging app, has evolved into a versatile platform for businesses. It offers a direct line of communication with customers, allowing for one-on-one interactions and personalized engagement. What sets WhatsApp apart is its reach; with billions of users worldwide, it's a global phenomenon. This extensive user base provides businesses with an unprecedented opportunity to connect with a diverse audience.

Additionally, WhatsApp's end-to-end encryption ensures that your conversations are secure, which can foster trust between your business and your customers. This trust forms the basis of strong, long-lasting relationships, making WhatsApp a suitable medium for businesses looking to build rapport and loyalty.

The multimedia capabilities of WhatsApp further enhance its utility. You can share not only text messages but also images, videos, documents, and even conduct voice and video calls. This versatility enables you to create engaging content and interact with your audience in various ways. In essence, WhatsApp is a powerhouse of potential for your business.

Understanding Your Audience

To effectively leverage WhatsApp for marketing, you must intimately understand your audience. This means gaining insights into their preferences, behaviors, and needs. A comprehensive understanding of your target demographic allows you to tailor your messages and offers to their specific interests.

Start by creating customer personas, which are fictional representations of your ideal customers. These personas can include details like age, gender, location, and preferences. By doing so, you'll have a clearer picture of who you are communicating with, and you can craft messages and content that resonate with them.

Furthermore, understanding your audience goes beyond demographics. It involves knowing their pain points, desires, and challenges. By empathizing with your audience, you can address their needs effectively and create messaging that truly speaks to them.

Defining Your Marketing Goals

Before embarking on your WhatsApp marketing journey, it's essential to establish clear and measurable marketing goals. What are you trying to achieve through WhatsApp? Do you want to boost sales, increase brand awareness, enhance customer support, or achieve some other objective? Defining these goals provides a roadmap for your marketing efforts.

Goals should be specific, measurable, achievable, relevant, and time-bound (SMART). For instance, if you aim to increase sales, you might set a goal to achieve a 20% boost in monthly sales within the next six months through WhatsApp marketing.

Having well-defined goals not only gives your marketing strategy direction but also allows you to track your progress. It's essential to periodically evaluate and adjust your goals to stay aligned with your business's evolving needs and objectives.

By understanding the power of WhatsApp for business, knowing your audience, and defining your marketing goals, you've laid the groundwork for a successful WhatsApp marketing campaign. These fundamental steps will serve as the building blocks for the strategies and techniques we'll explore in the subsequent chapters.

Chapter 2

Getting Started with WhatsApp Business

Considering the practical aspects of WhatsApp Business, you will be guided through the process of creating your account, setting up your profile, and providing an overview of the essential features that WhatsApp Business offers.

Creating a WhatsApp Business Account

To kickstart your WhatsApp marketing journey, you'll need a WhatsApp Business account. It's important to note that WhatsApp Business is a separate app from the standard WhatsApp Messenger, designed specifically for businesses. If you don't already have a WhatsApp Business account, you can download it from the app store and install it on your smartphone.

Once installed, follow the on-screen prompts to set up your business profile. You'll be asked to provide essential information such as your business name, logo, contact details, and a brief description. Ensure that the information you enter accurately represents your business, as this will be the first impression you make on your potential customers.

Setting Up Your Profile

Your WhatsApp Business profile is akin to your digital storefront. It's the first thing customers see when they engage with your business on WhatsApp. A well-optimized profile can make a significant difference in how customers perceive your business. Here's what you should focus on:

1. Business Name and Logo: Choose a clear and recognizable business name, and use a professional logo. Consistency in branding across all channels is key.

2. About Your Business: In the "About" section, provide a brief and engaging description of your business. This should give users an idea of what your business is all about.

3. Contact Information: Ensure that your contact information is up to date, including your phone number and email address. Customers need a way to reach you.

4. Business Hours: Specify your operating hours to manage customer expectations regarding response times.

5. Location: If applicable, you can add your physical address, which is especially useful for local businesses.

6. Website and Social Media Links: Include links to your website and social media profiles for additional engagement opportunities.

WhatsApp Business Features Overview

WhatsApp Business comes equipped with a set of features tailored to enhance your interactions with customers. Here's a brief overview of some key features:

1. Labels: Labels allow you to organize and categorize your chats, making it easier to manage and prioritize conversations. For instance, you can label chats as "New Leads" or "Customer Support."

2. Quick Replies: Quick replies enable you to create and save frequently used responses, saving you time when addressing common customer queries.

3. Automated Greetings: You can set up automated welcome messages to greet customers when they first message you. These greetings can be customized to provide specific information or offers.

4. Away Messages: When you're unavailable, you can set up messages to inform customers about your absence and when they can expect a response.

5. Messaging Statistics: WhatsApp Business offers insights into the performance of your messages, helping you track important metrics like message delivery, read receipts, and response times.

Getting started with WhatsApp Business is the foundation of your WhatsApp marketing journey. Your profile is your virtual business card, and the features at your disposal can streamline your customer interactions and make your business more efficient. In the following chapters, we'll explore how to make the most of these features to drive your sales and marketing efforts.

Chapter 3

Building Your Contact List

Your WhatsApp marketing journey hinges on having a robust and responsive contact list. Let's look into the strategies for collecting and organizing contacts, the importance of permission-based marketing, and how to leverage your existing customer databases to kickstart your WhatsApp marketing.

Collecting and Organizing Contacts

To effectively use WhatsApp for marketing, you'll need a list of contacts that have opted in to receive your messages. Building this list begins with your existing customer base and expands to new leads and potential customers. Here's how to collect and organize your contacts:

1. Customer Opt-In: Encourage your existing customers to opt in for WhatsApp updates. This can be done through various channels, such as your website, email newsletters, and social media. Make the process clear and straightforward, and ensure that customers know what kind of messages to expect.

2. Lead Generation: Utilize your website and landing pages to collect contact information from potential customers. Offer incentives like discounts, exclusive content, or free trials to entice visitors to subscribe.

3. QR Codes: Generate WhatsApp QR codes that customers can scan to instantly connect with your business. Place these codes on promotional materials, business cards, or in physical store locations.

4. Events and Trade Shows: If you attend industry events or trade shows, encourage attendees to join your WhatsApp list for real-time updates and exclusive offers.

5. Organize Your List: Segment your contact list into categories that make sense for your business. For example, you might have segments like "Newsletter Subscribers," "Recent Customers," or "VIP Members." This segmentation will allow you to send more targeted and relevant messages.

Permission-Based Marketing: Best Practices

Respect and compliance are at the core of permission-based marketing. Here are some best practices to keep in mind:

1. Double Opt-In: Implement a double opt-in process to confirm that users genuinely want to receive messages from your business. This ensures that your list is populated with engaged and interested users.

2. Clear Opt-Out Option: Make it easy for users to opt out of your WhatsApp list at any time. Including clear instructions in your messages for how to unsubscribe is a good practice.

3. Frequency and Relevance: Don't inundate your audience with messages. Send messages at a frequency that aligns with your customers' expectations and preferences. Additionally, ensure your messages are relevant to the recipient's interests.

4. Compliance with Regulations: Be aware of and adhere to data protection regulations like GDPR. It's crucial to obtain and handle user data in compliance with applicable laws.

Leveraging Existing Customer Databases

Your existing customer databases are a goldmine for WhatsApp marketing. Whether you have email lists, CRM databases, or phone numbers, you can leverage this information to jumpstart your WhatsApp contact list. Here's how:

1. Import Contacts: Many WhatsApp Business tools allow you to import contacts from external sources. Ensure that you have the necessary permissions and consent to use this data for WhatsApp marketing.

2. Cross-Promotion: Promote your WhatsApp channel to your email subscribers or social media followers. Let them know about the exclusive content or offers they can expect by joining your WhatsApp list.

3. Customer Segmentation: When importing contacts, segment them according to their relationship with your business. This helps you send personalized messages that are more likely to resonate with each group.

Building a robust contact list is the foundation of successful WhatsApp marketing. It's essential to do so in a compliant and ethical manner, respecting user preferences and privacy. By following these practices and leveraging your existing customer data, you'll be well on your way to creating a valuable list of engaged WhatsApp contacts.

Chapter 4

Crafting Compelling Messages

We are going into the art of crafting effective messages for WhatsApp marketing, exploring the principles of creating messages that engage your audience, the power of multimedia messaging, and the techniques for writing persuasive call-to-actions.

The Art of Effective Messaging

Creating effective messages on WhatsApp involves a mix of art and science. Here's how to master the art of effective messaging:

Clarity: Start with a clear and concise message. Avoid ambiguity and ensure that your audience instantly understands your message's purpose.

Personalization: Address your recipients by their name whenever possible. Personalization helps establish a connection and makes the message feel more relevant.

Value Proposition: Communicate the value of your message. Why should the recipient care? Whether it's a special offer, informative content, or a solution to a problem, make the value clear.

Relevance: Tailor your messages to the recipient's preferences and past interactions with your business. A message that aligns with their interests is more likely to engage.

Timing: Send messages at the right time. Consider your audience's time zone and daily routines to maximize the chances of your message being seen promptly.

Conversational Tone: Keep your messages conversational and approachable. WhatsApp is a personal messaging platform, and overly formal language can feel out of place.

Multimedia Messaging: Images, Videos, and More

Multimedia messages are a powerful tool in WhatsApp marketing. They capture attention, convey information effectively, and make your messages more engaging. Here's how to make the most of multimedia:

Images: Use images to showcase products, tell stories, or illustrate key points. High-quality images that align with your brand's aesthetics can leave a lasting impression.

Videos: Videos can provide in-depth explanations, showcase product demos, or tell a compelling story. Keep videos short and engaging to maintain the viewer's interest.

GIFs: Animated GIFs can add a touch of fun and playfulness to your messages. They're great for quick reactions or expressing emotions.

Documents and PDFs: Share documents like brochures, catalogs, or guides. These are valuable for sharing detailed information.

Audio Messages: Use audio messages for a more personal touch. They can convey emotions and tone that text alone might miss.

Interactive Elements: Utilize interactive features like buttons to direct recipients to specific actions, such as visiting your website, making a purchase, or participating in a survey.

Writing Persuasive Call-to-Actions

A call-to-action (CTA) is a critical element in your WhatsApp marketing messages. It tells the recipient what you want them to do next. Crafting persuasive CTAs involves the following strategies:

1. Be Clear and Direct: Make it evident what action you want the recipient to take. Whether it's "Shop Now," "Learn More," or "Subscribe Today," clarity is key.

2. Create a Sense of Urgency: Encourage immediate action by adding a time-sensitive element to your CTA. Phrases like "Limited Time Offer" or "Act Now" can prompt quicker responses.

3. Highlight Benefits: Emphasize the benefits of taking the desired action. Explain how it will solve a problem or fulfill a need.

4. Keep it Concise: CTAs should be concise and to the point. Short and impactful phrases are more effective.

5. Use Action Verbs: Employ action-oriented verbs that prompt the recipient to act. Words like "get," "download," "buy," or "join" work well.

6. Test and Iterate: Don't be afraid to test different CTAs to see which ones resonate best with your audience. Continuous refinement is crucial for optimizing your messaging strategy.

Crafting compelling messages on WhatsApp is an art that requires careful consideration of content, format, and delivery. By following these guidelines and experimenting with different approaches, you can create messages that captivate your audience, leverage multimedia effectively, and drive desired actions with persuasive call-to-actions.

Chapter 5

Segmenting Your Audience

Segmenting your audience is a crucial aspect of WhatsApp marketing. The importance of grouping contacts for targeted messaging, the significance of personalization and customization, and the essential practices for avoiding spammy behavior will be discussed.

Grouping Contacts for Targeted Messaging

Grouping your contacts into segments allows you to send more relevant and targeted messages. It's a strategic approach to ensure that your content aligns with the specific interests and needs of different subsets of your audience. Here's how to effectively group your contacts:

Demographics:

Consider creating segments based on demographic data, such as age, gender, location, or occupation. This information helps you craft messages that resonate with specific groups.

Behavioral Data:

Segment based on user behavior, such as past purchases, interaction with your previous messages, or engagement with your content. Tailor your messages to their behavior to increase relevance.

Preferences:

Ask your subscribers about their preferences during the opt-in process. You can then create segments based on their stated interests, ensuring that they receive content that aligns with what they've indicated.

Purchase History:

Segment your audience by their purchase history. This is particularly useful for e-commerce businesses. Send product recommendations, discounts, or updates based on their past purchases.

Engagement Levels:

Group your contacts based on their engagement levels. Prioritize sending messages to highly engaged users who are more likely to respond and convert.

Personalization and Customization

Personalization and customization are key to making your audience feel valued and heard. They help build stronger connections and trust between your business and your customers. Here's how to apply personalization and customization in your WhatsApp marketing:

Use First Names: Address your recipients by their first names whenever possible. This simple touch adds a personal element to your messages.

Tailored Content: Customize your messages to align with the specific segment or individual you're addressing. For example, if you have a segment of customers interested in a particular product category, send them relevant product updates.

Behavior-Driven Personalization: If a user has interacted with your messages in a certain way, such as clicking on specific links or viewing particular content, use this data to send them more of what they've shown interest in.

Location-Based Content: Customize messages based on the recipient's location. Send location-specific promotions or event announcements.

User History: Refer to the recipient's history with your business. If they've recently made a purchase, acknowledge it in your message and offer complementary products or services.

Conversational Style: Personalization can also involve adopting a conversational style that aligns with the recipient's past interactions. For instance, if a customer has a friendly tone, maintain that tone in your responses.

Avoiding Spammy Behavior

WhatsApp users value their privacy and don't appreciate intrusive or spammy behavior. To maintain a positive reputation and ensure compliance with WhatsApp's policies, follow these best practices:

1. Permission-Based Messaging: Only send messages to users who have opted in to receive them. Unsolicited messages can be considered spam.

2. Respect Unsubscribes: Honor unsubscribe requests promptly. If a user wishes to opt out, make the process easy and ensure they no longer receive messages.

3. Frequency Control: Avoid bombarding users with frequent messages. Striking the right balance between staying engaged and being intrusive is essential.

4. Clear Identification: Always identify your business in messages. Users should know who is contacting them.

5. Relevancy: Ensure that the messages you send are relevant to the recipient's interests or past interactions. Irrelevant messages can be seen as spam.

Segmentation, personalization, and avoiding spammy behavior are interconnected aspects of WhatsApp marketing that play a critical role in building positive customer relationships and achieving better results from your messaging efforts. By putting these principles into practice, you can create more engaging, targeted, and compliant campaigns.

Chapter 6

Automation and Chatbots

Automation and chatbots are essential tools in your WhatsApp marketing arsenal, helping you streamline customer engagement, save time, and provide efficient responses. Introducing the concept of automation, using chatbots for customer engagement, and providing guidance on implementing automated responses will be explained.

Automation

Automation in WhatsApp marketing refers to the process of using technology to perform tasks and actions without human intervention. It allows you to scale your communication efforts, provide timely responses, and maintain consistency in your messaging. Here's why automation is important:

1. Efficiency: Automation can handle routine tasks, freeing up your time to focus on more strategic aspects of your business.

2. Consistency: Automated processes ensure that every customer receives the same quality of service and information.

3. Timeliness: Automated responses can be instant, improving the customer experience by providing quick answers to queries.

4. Scalability: As your contact list grows, automation enables you to handle a larger volume of interactions without increasing your workload.

Using Chatbots for Customer Engagement

Chatbots are a specific form of automation that can engage with customers in a conversational manner. They can be programmed to perform a variety of tasks, from answering frequently asked questions to guiding users through product recommendations. Here's how to effectively use chatbots for customer engagement on WhatsApp:

1. Customer Support: Implement chatbots to handle common customer support inquiries. They can provide quick resolutions to issues like password resets, order tracking, or FAQs.

2. Lead Qualification: Chatbots can ask qualifying questions to leads and direct them to the appropriate sales team or offer more detailed information based on their responses.

3. Appointment Scheduling: Use chatbots to facilitate appointment scheduling. They can check your availability and book appointments seamlessly.

4. Product Recommendations: Based on user preferences and behavior, chatbots can suggest products or services that match their interests.

5. Survey and Feedback Collection: Chatbots can gather user feedback through surveys and analyze responses to improve your services.

6. Interactive Content: Create interactive content experiences with chatbots, such as quizzes, polls, or contests, to engage and entertain your audience.

Implementing Automated Responses

Automated responses are a core component of automation in WhatsApp marketing. They ensure that your audience receives immediate feedback and assistance. Here's how to implement automated responses effectively:

1. Welcome Messages: Set up welcome messages to greet users when they first contact your business. These messages can introduce your business, provide contact details, and offer options for assistance.

2. Frequently Asked Questions (FAQs): Create automated responses for common FAQs. This ensures that users receive answers to their questions without delay.

3. Response Time Expectations: Inform users about your response time expectations. Automated messages can manage user expectations and provide transparency.

4. Away Messages: Use away messages when you're unavailable. These messages inform users about your unavailability and when they can expect a response.

5. Multi-Language Support: If your audience is diverse, consider implementing automated responses in multiple languages to cater to a broader user base.

6. Customization: While automation is powerful, ensure that your automated responses maintain a human touch and the ability to direct users to human agents for more complex inquiries.

Automation and chatbots are invaluable tools for enhancing customer engagement, efficiency, and scalability in your WhatsApp marketing strategy. When properly implemented, they can deliver a seamless user experience and improve your ability to serve your audience effectively.

Chapter 7

Creating Engaging Content

Let's take a keen look at the art of creating engaging content for WhatsApp marketing. We'll critically look into the development of a content strategy tailored for WhatsApp, the use of contests and giveaways to boost engagement, and effective storytelling techniques to captivate your audience.

Content Strategy for WhatsApp

A well-defined content strategy is the backbone of successful WhatsApp marketing. It involves planning, creating, and distributing content that aligns with your business objectives and resonates with your audience. This is how to create an effective content strategy for WhatsApp:

Identify Your Goals
- Start by defining your marketing goals. Are you looking to drive sales, build brand awareness, provide customer support, or achieve other objectives? Your content strategy should align with these goals.

Understand Your Audience
- Thoroughly understand your audience's needs, preferences, and pain points. This knowledge will guide the type of content you create and how you deliver it.

Content Types

- Determine the types of content that best suit your audience and objectives. This can include text messages, images, videos, GIFs, audio messages, documents, and more.

Content Calendar

- Develop a content calendar outlining the timing and frequency of your messages. Consistency is key in keeping your audience engaged.

Value-Driven Content

- Ensure that your content provides value to your audience. Inform, educate, entertain, or solve their problems. Valuable content builds trust and keeps users engaged.

Personalization

- Customize your content for different segments of your audience. Personalized content is more likely to resonate with users.

Testing and Optimization

- Continuously test your content and analyze its performance. Use insights to refine your strategy and make data-driven decisions.

Running Contests and Giveaways

Contests and giveaways are excellent engagement boosters in WhatsApp marketing. They create excitement, encourage participation, and offer incentives for users to interact with your business. Here's how to effectively run contests and giveaways on WhatsApp:

1. Clear Objectives: Define clear objectives for your contests or giveaways. Are you looking to increase brand awareness, collect user-generated content, or boost sales? Knowing your goals will shape your strategy.

2. Prizes and Incentives: Offer prizes that are appealing to your target audience. Ensure that the rewards are relevant and valuable to participants.

3. Simple Participation: Keep participation simple and accessible. Complicated entry requirements can deter users from taking part.

4. Clear Rules: Clearly outline the rules and terms of the contest or giveaway. Transparency is crucial to build trust.

5. Promotion: Promote your contest or giveaway through your other marketing channels, such as social media, email, and your website, to maximize participation.

6. Engagement and Interactivity: Engage with participants throughout the contest to keep the excitement alive. Respond to questions, acknowledge entries, and announce winners promptly.

7. User-Generated Content: Encourage participants to create content, such as photos or videos, as part of the contest. This content can be repurposed in your future marketing efforts.

Storytelling Techniques

Storytelling is a powerful tool for creating emotional connections with your audience. Effective storytelling can make your WhatsApp marketing content more relatable and memorable. Here are some storytelling techniques to apply:

1. Character Development: Introduce relatable characters or personas in your stories. These characters can embody your brand and engage with your audience on a personal level.

2. Conflict and Resolution: Engage your audience with stories that present conflicts and resolutions. This structure keeps users hooked as they anticipate how the story unfolds.

3. Emotion and Empathy: Stir emotions through your stories. Share experiences that elicit empathy, joy, or even challenges that your audience can relate to.

4. Visual Storytelling: Use multimedia elements to enhance your storytelling. Combine text with images or videos to create a more immersive experience.

5. Consistency: Maintain a consistent narrative and tone in your storytelling. Consistency helps build your brand's story over time.

6. Call-to-Action: Conclude your story with a clear call-to-action, directing users on what they should do next.

Creating engaging content, running contests and giveaways, and using storytelling techniques can significantly enhance your WhatsApp marketing efforts. Content that resonates with your audience, provides value, and encourages interaction can boost your brand's presence and drive meaningful engagement.

Chapter 8

Running Promotions and Campaigns

Running promotions and campaigns on WhatsApp can be a potent way to drive sales, engage with your audience, and achieve specific marketing objectives. The strategies for using discounts, coupons, and flash sales, the importance of measuring the success of your campaigns, and provide insights through case studies of successful WhatsApp campaigns are the base of this chapter.

Discounts, Coupons, and Flash Sales

Offering discounts, coupons, and flash sales through WhatsApp can create excitement and drive conversions. Here's how to use these promotions effectively:

1. Discounts: Discounts can be offered as a percentage off the regular price, a fixed amount reduction, or buy-one-get-one (BOGO) deals. Make sure the discount is significant enough to motivate action.

2. Coupons: Provide exclusive coupon codes to your WhatsApp subscribers. These codes can be used during online checkout or presented in-store for discounts.

3. Flash Sales: Create a sense of urgency with flash sales. These are short-duration sales with limited quantities of products at a reduced price. Use compelling messaging to announce the flash sale and its end time to prompt quick action.

4. Personalization: Tailor your offers to the preferences and behavior of your WhatsApp contacts. Send discounts or coupons for products or services they've shown interest in.

5. Promotion Announcements: Promote your discounts, coupons, or flash sales with eye-catching and informative messages, including images or videos of the featured products.

6. Countdowns and Reminders: Send countdown messages leading up to the start of a flash sale, and reminders just before it ends to create a sense of urgency.

Measuring the Success of Campaigns

Measuring the success of your WhatsApp marketing campaigns is crucial to understand their impact and make data-driven improvements. Key metrics to monitor include:

Click-Through Rate (CTR)
- Measure the percentage of recipients who clicked on your campaign messages or links.

Conversion Rate
- Track how many recipients completed the desired action after engaging with your campaign, such as making a purchase.

Engagement Rate
- Assess how many users interacted with your campaign content, including likes, shares, and comments.

Response Rate
- Monitor the percentage of users who responded to your campaign messages. A higher response rate can indicate strong engagement.

ROI (Return on Investment)
- Calculate the return on investment by comparing the cost of the campaign to the revenue generated as a result of it.

Customer Feedback
- Collect user feedback to gauge their satisfaction and gather insights for future campaigns.

Subscriber Growth
- Analyze how your campaign affected your WhatsApp subscriber list. Did you see an increase in subscribers during or after the campaign?

Case Studies of Successful WhatsApp Campaigns

Real-world case studies provide valuable insights into effective WhatsApp campaigns. Here are a couple of examples:

E-commerce Flash Sale

- An online fashion retailer ran a flash sale exclusively for its WhatsApp subscribers. They sent out enticing messages with images of the discounted items and a clear countdown. The campaign resulted in a 50% increase in sales over the sale period.

Restaurant Coupons

- A restaurant chain offered a special WhatsApp coupon for a free dessert with the purchase of a main course. The coupon was redeemable in-store by showing it to the staff. This campaign not only increased foot traffic but also helped build their WhatsApp subscriber list.

These case studies demonstrate how the strategic use of discounts, coupons, and flash sales can lead to tangible results, such as increased sales, user engagement, and subscriber growth.

Running promotions and campaigns on WhatsApp can be a potent strategy for achieving marketing goals, but it's essential to measure their success and refine your approach based on the data and feedback you gather. Effective campaigns can make a significant impact on your business's growth and customer engagement.

Chapter 9

Analytics and Performance Tracking

Monitoring and analyzing the performance of your WhatsApp marketing efforts is crucial for making informed decisions and optimizing your strategy. We'll look at the process of monitoring WhatsApp marketing metrics, adjusting your strategy based on data, and introduce tools for WhatsApp analytics.

Monitoring Your WhatsApp Marketing Metrics

To track the effectiveness of your WhatsApp marketing campaigns, you should keep a close eye on the following key metrics:

1. Message Delivery Rate: This metric indicates the percentage of messages successfully delivered to your recipients. A high delivery rate is essential for ensuring that your content reaches your audience.

2. Read Receipts: It's important to know how many of your messages are actually being read. Read receipts provide insights into the engagement level of your audience.

3. Response Rate: The response rate measures how often recipients interact with your messages by replying or taking the desired action. A high response rate signifies engagement.

4. Click-Through Rate (CTR): For campaigns that include links, tracking the CTR reveals how many recipients clicked on the provided links. This metric is especially valuable for evaluating the effectiveness of your calls-to-action.

5. Conversion Rate: If your goal is to drive conversions (e.g., sales or sign-ups), monitoring the conversion rate helps you understand how many recipients completed the desired action after interacting with your messages.

6. Subscriber Growth: Keep an eye on how your subscriber list is growing over time. Monitoring this metric allows you to assess the effectiveness of your subscription strategies.

7. Engagement Metrics: Analyze likes, shares, and comments to gauge the level of engagement and interaction with your content.

Adjusting Your Strategy Based on Data

Once you've collected data on your WhatsApp marketing performance, it's essential to adjust your strategy accordingly. How to make data-driven improvements:

1. Identify Strong and Weak Areas: Analyze which aspects of your campaigns are performing well and which ones are underperforming. Are

certain types of content more engaging? Are specific campaigns delivering better results?

2. A/B Testing: Conduct A/B tests to experiment with variations in your messaging, such as different images, content, or call-to-actions. Use the results to refine your approach.

3. Optimize Timing: Use insights to determine when your audience is most active and responsive on WhatsApp. Adjust your messaging schedule to maximize engagement during these times.

4. Segmentation Refinement: If certain segments of your audience are more responsive than others, consider further segmenting your list to provide more targeted content.

5. Content Adjustments: Make content improvements based on user feedback and metrics. If specific types of content consistently receive higher engagement, focus on creating more of it.

6. ROI Assessment: Continuously evaluate the return on investment for your WhatsApp marketing efforts. Adjust your spending and resource allocation based on the campaigns that deliver the best ROI.

Tools for WhatsApp Analytics

There are various tools and platforms available to help you monitor and analyze your WhatsApp marketing metrics. Here are a few notable options:

1. WhatsApp Business API: WhatsApp's own API provides insights into message delivery, read receipts, and response rates.

2. Google Analytics: You can integrate Google Analytics to track website traffic originating from your WhatsApp campaigns. This helps you understand how WhatsApp contributes to your online performance.

3. Third-Party Analytics Tools: Several third-party tools offer advanced analytics features specifically designed for WhatsApp marketing. These tools often provide more detailed insights and reporting options.

4. Custom Tracking URLs: Use custom tracking URLs to monitor the effectiveness of links in your WhatsApp messages. Tools like Bitly or UTM parameters can help with this.

By continually monitoring your WhatsApp marketing metrics, you can make informed decisions, optimize your strategies, and ensure that your efforts align with your goals. Data-driven adjustments are key to achieving better results and maximizing the impact of your WhatsApp marketing campaigns.

Chapter 10

Compliance and Privacy

Compliance with WhatsApp policies, user privacy, and data protection are critical aspects of WhatsApp marketing. Let's focus together on the importance of staying compliant with WhatsApp policies, the significance of user privacy, and how the General Data Protection Regulation (GDPR) relates to WhatsApp marketing.

Staying Compliant with WhatsApp Policies

WhatsApp has specific policies and guidelines that businesses must adhere to when using the platform for marketing. It's crucial to understand and comply with these policies to maintain a positive reputation and avoid potential penalties or account restrictions. Here are some key aspects of WhatsApp policies to consider:

1. Permission-Based Marketing: Always obtain explicit consent from users before sending them marketing messages on WhatsApp. Users should have the choice to opt in or opt out at any time.

2. Business Verification: Businesses must complete a verification process to confirm their identity and authenticity. Verified businesses are more trusted by users.

3. No Spam or Automated Bulk Messaging: WhatsApp strictly prohibits spammy behavior and automated bulk messaging. Unsolicited messages or excessive messaging can lead to account suspension.

4. Data Protection: Ensure that you handle user data in accordance with data protection laws and user privacy rights. Protect user data and use it responsibly.

5. User Rights: Respect user rights, including the right to access their data, the right to be forgotten, and the right to data portability.

User Privacy and Data Protection

User privacy is paramount when it comes to WhatsApp marketing. Respecting user privacy builds trust and encourages users to engage with your business. These are some best practices to prioritize user privacy in your WhatsApp marketing:

1. Data Minimization: Collect and store only the data necessary for your marketing activities. Avoid gathering excessive information about users.

2. Security Measures: Implement robust security measures to protect user data. Ensure that data is encrypted and stored securely.

3. Consent Mechanisms: Use clear and transparent mechanisms to obtain user consent for data processing. Make it easy for users to opt in or opt out of marketing messages.

4. Data Retention: Define data retention policies that determine how long you keep user data. Data should be retained only for the necessary duration.

5. Transparency: Be transparent about how you collect, use, and store user data. Provide clear privacy policies and information about your data practices.

6. Data Transfer: If you transfer user data between countries, ensure it complies with international data transfer regulations, such as GDPR.

GDPR and WhatsApp Marketing

The General Data Protection Regulation (GDPR) is a comprehensive data protection regulation in the European Union. If you engage in WhatsApp marketing and have EU users in your contact list, you must ensure GDPR compliance. Here are some considerations:

1. Data Collection: Obtain explicit consent from EU users for data collection and processing. This includes capturing their WhatsApp numbers and any other personal information.

2. Data Portability: Users have the right to request their data from you. Ensure you can provide users with their data in a commonly used format upon request.

3. Right to Be Forgotten: Users have the right to request the deletion of their data. You must have processes in place to fulfill these requests promptly.

4. Data Transfer: If you transfer user data outside the EU, make sure it's done in compliance with GDPR regulations. Consider using Standard Contractual Clauses (SCCs) or other legally recognized mechanisms.

5. Data Protection Impact Assessments (DPIAs): If you engage in high-risk data processing activities, such as profiling or large-scale processing, conduct DPIAs to assess and mitigate risks to user data.

Compliance with WhatsApp policies and privacy regulations like GDPR is not just a legal obligation but also an ethical responsibility. It demonstrates your commitment to protecting user data and maintaining their trust, which is essential for successful WhatsApp marketing.

Chapter 11

Troubleshooting and Problem Solving

WhatsApp marketing, like any other marketing channel, can come with its share of challenges. Common challenges in WhatsApp marketing and pro with solutions for technical and engagement issues. How to effectively deal with unsubscribers and negative feedback.

Common Challenges in WhatsApp Marketing

1. Low Engagement: One of the most common challenges is low engagement. If your messages are not generating responses, it may be due to uninteresting content, improper timing, or a lack of personalization.

2. Technical Issues: Technical glitches can hamper your WhatsApp marketing efforts. These might include delivery issues, message formatting problems, or account verification delays.

3. Privacy Concerns: Some users may be concerned about their privacy when receiving messages from businesses on WhatsApp. Overcoming these concerns can be a challenge.

4. Unsubscribers: Users opting out of your messages can be discouraging. Understanding why they're unsubscribing and minimizing this number is a common challenge.

5. Negative Feedback: Negative feedback, whether through responses or online reviews, can affect your brand's reputation. Managing this feedback is essential.

Solutions for Technical and Engagement Issues

1. Content Optimization: To improve engagement, focus on creating more engaging and personalized content. Use multimedia elements, storytelling, and clear call-to-actions to prompt user interaction.

2. Technical Support: Reach out to WhatsApp's technical support for help with any account or delivery issues. They can assist in resolving technical glitches and ensuring the smooth functioning of your WhatsApp Business account.

3. Privacy Transparency: Address privacy concerns by clearly communicating your data handling practices. Provide information about how you protect user data and why your messages are valuable.

4. Test and Learn: Experiment with different content, timing, and messaging strategies to understand what works best with your audience. Continuously test and refine your approach.

5. Segmentation: Improve engagement by segmenting your audience and delivering more targeted content to different groups. Tailored messages are more likely to resonate with users.

Dealing with Unsubscribers and Negative Feedback

1. Collect Feedback: When users unsubscribe or provide negative feedback, use the opportunity to collect valuable insights. Ask for feedback on why they're opting out or what didn't meet their expectations.

2. Re-Engagement Campaigns: Implement re-engagement campaigns for subscribers who have become less active or have shown signs of disengagement. Offer them incentives or exclusive content to encourage re-engagement.

3. Professional Responses: When dealing with negative feedback, respond professionally and empathetically. Address their concerns, offer solutions, and strive to turn a negative experience into a positive one.

4. Data Privacy Compliance: Ensure that you're fully compliant with data protection regulations. Show your commitment to user privacy by maintaining transparent and secure data handling practices.

5. Educate and Inform: Regularly educate your subscribers about the value of your messages and why they subscribed in the first place. Remind them of the benefits of staying subscribed.

6. Continuous Improvement: Act on the feedback you receive to improve your WhatsApp marketing strategy. By addressing issues and evolving your approach, you can minimize unsubscribers and negative feedback over time.

Challenges in WhatsApp marketing are common, but they are also opportunities for growth and improvement. By addressing these challenges with proactive solutions, continuous learning, and a commitment to user satisfaction, you can build a more effective and successful WhatsApp marketing strategy.

Chapter 12

Future Trends and Innovations

As WhatsApp marketing continues to evolve, it's essential for businesses to anticipate future trends and prepare for emerging technologies to stay competitive and relevant. Current trends and predictions for the future of WhatsApp marketing, offering guidance on preparing for emerging technologies, and discussing strategies for staying ahead of the curve.

Predictions for the Future of WhatsApp Marketing

1. AI-Enhanced Customer Service: Artificial intelligence (AI) will play a significant role in improving customer service on WhatsApp. Chatbots will become even more sophisticated, offering real-time support and assistance. AI will also power predictive analytics, helping businesses better understand and serve their customers.

2. Integration with E-commerce: WhatsApp's potential as an e-commerce platform will continue to expand. Businesses will be able to showcase their products and services more effectively, offer in-app purchases, and provide seamless transaction experiences for customers.

3. Video and Multimedia: The importance of video and multimedia content in WhatsApp marketing will grow. Short video messages, product demos,

and interactive multimedia content will be used to engage users and convey information more effectively.

4. Personalization and Data-Driven Marketing: Advances in data analytics and AI will enable businesses to offer highly personalized marketing messages. Targeted and relevant content will become the norm, driving higher engagement and conversion rates.

5. Richer Conversational Experiences: Conversations on WhatsApp will become richer, with features like interactive buttons, forms, and mini-applications. This will enhance user engagement and streamline interactions.

6. Privacy-Centric Marketing: Privacy concerns will remain a top priority. Businesses will need to be transparent about data handling practices, adhere to data protection regulations, and gain user trust through responsible data use.

Preparing for Emerging Technologies

1. AI Adoption: Businesses should consider integrating AI and chatbots into their WhatsApp marketing strategy. Invest in AI-powered tools that enhance customer service and automate routine tasks. Stay updated on AI advancements and best practices.

2. E-commerce Optimization: If applicable to your business, prepare for e-commerce integration on WhatsApp. Ensure that your product catalog and payment systems are well-prepared for in-app transactions.

3. Video Content Creation: Develop the skills or collaborate with professionals for creating compelling video content. Understand how to use video for product demonstrations, storytelling, and interactive experiences.

4. Data Analysis and Personalization: Invest in data analysis tools to harness the potential of AI-driven personalization. Build a customer database that allows for highly targeted marketing campaigns.

5. Interactive Content: Explore the creation of interactive content. Learn how to implement features like interactive buttons and forms within WhatsApp to enhance user engagement.

6. Privacy and Compliance: Stay informed about data protection regulations and ensure your data handling practices are in compliance. Prioritize user privacy and maintain transparency in your communications.

Staying Ahead of the Curve

To remain at the forefront of WhatsApp marketing, adopt a culture of continuous learning and adaptation:

1. Stay Informed: Keep up with industry news and trends through blogs, podcasts, and industry publications. Attend webinars, conferences, and workshops to gain valuable insights.

2. Benchmark Successful Campaigns: Study successful WhatsApp marketing campaigns and businesses in your niche. Extract inspiration and learn from their strategies and innovations.

3. Embrace Innovation: Foster a mindset of innovation within your team. Be open to testing new strategies and technologies, and encourage a culture of creative problem-solving.

4. Collaboration: Collaborate with professionals who specialize in emerging technologies and marketing strategies. Seek partnerships and alliances that can drive innovation in your WhatsApp marketing efforts.

5. Prioritize User Privacy: As you explore new horizons in WhatsApp marketing, always prioritize user privacy and data protection. Adherence to privacy standards builds trust with your audience.

By staying informed, embracing innovation, and adhering to best practices, you'll be well-prepared to navigate the ever-evolving landscape of WhatsApp marketing. Keep your finger on the pulse of emerging technologies and trends, and be ready to adapt your strategies to leverage the full potential of WhatsApp as a marketing platform.

Recap of Key Notes

In the ever-evolving world of digital marketing, WhatsApp has emerged as a powerful platform for businesses to connect with their audience. Throughout this ebook, we've explored the essential strategies, techniques, and best practices for WhatsApp marketing. Let's recap the key takeaways and provide you with a clear roadmap to WhatsApp marketing success.

Key Notes

1. Permission is Paramount: Always obtain explicit consent from users before sending them marketing messages on WhatsApp. Permission-based marketing is not only ethical but also ensures that your audience is receptive to your messages.

2. Business Verification: Complete the verification process to establish trust with your audience. A verified WhatsApp Business account is more likely to be seen as legitimate.

3. Content is King: Create engaging, valuable, and personalized content that resonates with your audience. Multimedia content, storytelling, and interactive elements can enhance engagement.

4. Segmentation Matters: Segment your audience to provide targeted content. Personalization leads to higher engagement and conversion rates.

5. Automation and Chatbots: Leverage automation and chatbots for efficient customer service and engagement. These tools can handle routine tasks and provide instant responses.

6. Data Privacy and Compliance: Prioritize user privacy and data protection. Comply with WhatsApp policies, GDPR, and other data protection regulations.

7. Measure and Adapt: Continuously monitor and analyze your WhatsApp marketing metrics. Make data-driven decisions, adjust your strategy based on insights, and strive for continuous improvement.

8. Prepare for the Future: Anticipate emerging trends and technologies in WhatsApp marketing. Stay ahead by investing in AI, video content, e-commerce integration, and interactive experiences.

Your Roadmap to WhatsApp Marketing Success

- Start with Permission:

Begin by building a permission-based subscriber list. Ensure that your audience has opted in to receive your messages.

- Content Strategy:

Develop a content strategy that focuses on delivering value to your audience. Create a content calendar and plan various content types, including text, images, videos, and interactive elements.

- Segmentation and Personalization:

Segment your audience based on their preferences and behaviors. Tailor your messages to each segment for a more personalized experience.

- Automation and Chatbots:

Implement automation and chatbots for customer support, efficiency, and consistency. Use them to streamline routine tasks and provide instant responses.

- Data Protection and Compliance:

Handle user data responsibly and in compliance with data protection regulations. Be transparent about your data practices and privacy policies.

- Analytics and Optimization:

Continuously monitor your WhatsApp marketing metrics. Analyze your campaigns, adjust your strategy, and strive for better performance and engagement.

- Prepare for the Future:

Stay informed about emerging technologies and trends in WhatsApp marketing. Invest in AI, video content, e-commerce integration, and interactive experiences to remain competitive.

- Innovate and Collaborate:

Foster a culture of innovation within your team. Collaborate with professionals who specialize in emerging technologies, and stay open to testing new strategies.

- Prioritize Privacy:

Throughout your journey in WhatsApp marketing, make user privacy a top priority. By respecting user data and adhering to privacy standards, you build trust and loyalty with your audience.

WhatsApp marketing holds immense potential for businesses to connect, engage, and convert their audience. With the right strategies and a commitment to user privacy, you can navigate the dynamic landscape of WhatsApp marketing successfully. Embrace the tools, techniques, and innovations that WhatsApp offers, and always strive to provide value to your subscribers. This roadmap will guide you on your journey to WhatsApp marketing success.

www.ingramcontent.com/pod-product-compliance
Lightning Source LLC
Chambersburg PA
CBHW061051050326
40690CB00012B/2581

* 9 7 9 8 8 6 4 5 4 6 1 4 7 *